FROM WHERE I SIT

Poems and Sketches from later years

KENNETH E. GRANT

authorHOUSE®

AuthorHouse™
1663 Liberty Drive
Bloomington, IN 47403
www.authorhouse.com
Phone: 1 (800) 839-8640

Published by AuthorHouse 09/06/2019

ISBN: 978-1-7283-2631-3 (sc)
ISBN: 978-1-7283-2632-0 (hc)
ISBN: 978-1-7283-2630-6 (e)

Library of Congress Control Number: 2019913308

Print information available on the last page.

This book is printed on acid-free paper.

DEDICATION

In memory of my brother Roderick Grant whose several
books of excellent poetry inspired this volume.

FOREWORD

The poems in this book might be called reflections of my later years. They reflect the variety of experiences life has offered and the many wonderful people I have been privileged to know. Each poem reflects the unique, emotional impact these experiences have made on this admittedly sentimental soul.

You will find the poems arranged into five sections, each with its own emphasis. Section one reflects the impact that the natural world has made on my life. The second, Along the Way, reflects the many dimensions life presents, its emotions and thoughts and often my response. The third reflects seasons of the year. Section four, Remembering, includes memories and those people and circumstances that created these special occasions. The last section, Senior Years, touches the many thoughts on life and some responses by those of us in our senior years.

In addition to the poems, I have added a section of sketches I have drawn over the years, many while recuperating from a recent illness. I have been sketching and drawing since I was a child.

I am no longer young. Senior readers, I suspect will identify readily with perspectives found here. You who are young, however, may find a glimpse into how your grandparents see their world and their life in it. It is by no means a gloomy picture, whatever its pain or pathos. This life and the world we live in are filled with incredible beauty, great mystery, and awesome wonder. Living fully means being open to it all, to share with our fellow travelers, to help them with their load; and allow them to help all of us who strive to leave this world with some gift of our presence. This book is intended to be a part of that gift.

CONTENTS

Section 1

Section 2

Section 3

Section 4

Section 5

Section 6

Section 1

Nature

IN SEARCH OF BEAUTY

Oh my
There are things
That ravage the eye
That catch the breath
That halt my footsteps
Simply because
They are exquisite
So altogether
Beautiful

No precise prediction
Of a time or place
For though a garden
Or a fragrant forest
May fling wide a gate
To such a time

Yet
Some ordinary day
In an ordinary place
Some common thing may
Suddenly
Catch the eye
Revealing a particular
Though hidden beauty
Quite undetected by the busy
And unseeing
Passer by

So it seems
Quite wise
To educate one's senses
To pause and gaze with
A more patient eye and
Listening ear
To catch the sights and sounds
The symphony
This amazing world each day
Is playing

For trees still sway to the music
Of whispering breeze
While flowers and grasses bow
As in
Joyful greeting

While our city streets
Cacophony provide
It's strike up the band
Sound the horns and
Let the trombones slide

Yet for strollers passing
There's no melody in traffic
And they can hardly wait
For the racket to subside

Still for all the noise and
Clamor that surrounds
Beauty remains hidden
In each day
If we but school ourselves to
Seek it
It is there for everyone
Waiting to be found

I LOVE THE COUNTRY

I love the air of country
Of hay and grass and flowers
Pungent with the scent of cows
After springtime showers

I love the sounds of country
The hum of bees and things
Of crickets singing in the night
The bubbling of a spring

I love the country faces
Alight with friendly smiles
Open, honest, down-home folk
With their own down-home style

I love the scenes of country
Fields and hills and sod
When little country churches stand
Pointing the way to God

And someday when I take leave
To bid this world goodby
I trust the Lord will welcome me
To his Country in the sky

THE LEAVES OF FALL

There is an edge to the breeze
A coolness lacking just
Days ago
The old tree in the yard
Whose leaves foretell the
Ever-changing seasons
Now begins to let them go
One by one
Then in glorious deluge
On grass below

And they fall
Not like leaden rocks
Shaken from trembling mountain
Awakened from ancient sleep
Nor as apples falling
From late Autumn's tree
But gracefully drifting down in
A lovely ballet
Turning, bowing, twisting, twirling
Ever descending in a
Glorious display
And the lawn beneath becomes a
Bright kaleidoscope
An Autumn grand finale
For the leaves of Fall
And the gift of an ancient tree

Ah but yes
The leaves signal more
To discerning eyes
Than art or season suggest

For their tenure through a season
Holding to a firmer bough
Is not unlike my mortal grip on
This world's daily provision

Or what earthly institutions
May provide
For as my mortal season nears
Its ending and as
Turning leaves remind
I shall someday lose my hold
On whatever mortal limb was mine
And with grateful heart join the
Great unseen assembly
That in its season and descending
Left its pattern
On the living grass

For we share with every life
The seasons as they turn
And when our Spring and
Summer days are over
A final Autumn waits us all
Yet by faith
We shall be trusting that
After winter slumber
Another and eternal Spring
Will come

MORNING COMES

Morning comes
Eventually
And not even a lack of
Sleep-graced hours
Can delay the
Silver edge of dawn
Or keep the lark from
Rising to the sun

So
I suppose
I should be rising too
To go about the things
It appears
That I should do

Singing like the lark
Has not been granted me
And
Flying's not an option
For featherless creatures
Lacking wings

Yet
A heart may fly
And spirits soar
And dreams give wings
To earthlings such as I
So that the lark
Need not soar alone

Morning has come
The day begun
The silver trumpets
Of the dawn
Sound their reveille

So
I shall rise
To do the things that lead
Up the winding path
To where
A dream
Lies waiting

SPRING'S ARRIVAL

Ah...
I believe it has arrived at last
Tho' snow still lingers in crevices
On mountain slopes
While a cool breeze breathes
Now and then
Bidding farewell as Winter departs

Opening buds and
Bursting blossoms
Host a cloud of buzzing bees
As all join to bid an arriving Spring
A colorful and fragrant welcome Uniting in a blessed balm
For winter weary hearts

The bird of paradise by
Our front porch
Shoots orange flame blossoms
Up through deep green leaves
Erupting as though rejoicing
From moist brown earth beneath
Refreshed by springtime showers

Reclining now
In languid springtime ease
Pondering more than
Mind can manage or pen record
I sigh
And note the shadows cast
By ancient oaks across the way
Dappling the lawn beneath with
Soft patches of gentle shade
And afternoon sunlight

But then
Butterflies and bees
Of many shapes and sizes
Fly by my languid observation
In amazing number
On their way no doubt
To feast in nectar gardens
Newly birthed by mother earth
In this bountiful Spring

Thus is born a prayer
That this season prove a balm
And birth a spring of hope
For those long suffering
A winter of despair

For the Birther of the springtime
Who brings the buds to flower
Can bring His Spring
To hurting hearts
With Son-lit love and kindness
And spread his Springtime
Everywhere

THE HEAT
A culinary comment...

Whew!
It's hot as
"All get out"
As the saying goes
And I do suppose
That you could no doubt
Fry an egg
Out on the sidewalk
In the sun
Although a bit of butter
On the spot
Before the shell is broke
Might help a bit
When time arrives
To scoop it up
When that misplaced egg
Is done

THE NIGHT

Quiet the velvet night
Birds sleep silent in their nests
While a billion stars keep watch
And a mystic moon
Hangs round and pale
Above the shadowed trees
At garden's edge

A soft night breeze
Breathes gently on my face
Whispers softly in the leaves
And then
Is still

A cricket
Tiny troubadour
In the grasses
Begins his serenade
As fireflies rise
To briefly glow
And
Disappear

So calm the night
Daytime clamor drained away
And it is time
To soak a daylight soul
In night's cool balm
And rest
To rise refreshed
And greet the sunrise of
Another dawn

THE STORM

Hush
Quiet
Listen!
The distance mumbles
A low growl
Deep in a distant throat
Then
An ominous quiet
Waiting
Wide eyed
Still

Again!
Nearer now
A chill wind begins
To worry the giant sycamore
Bend the grass and
bow the garden flowers
Rippling the surface of
The pond

Suddenly
A thousand cannons roar!
The bass drums of the sky roll
Sounding the storm's arrival
The denouement of
The sky's dark demon
Savaging the earth with
Sweeping sheets of rain
Pelting roof tops
Pounding hapless autos with
merciless bombardments
Of icy hail

Then
Suddenly
Subsiding
The rolling thunder
Moves on east
The assault subsides
Leaving the town
The flooded streets and
Wounded garden
Where droops the
Shredded sycamore
To slowly resurrect
And bless a
Bright
Returning
Sun

TINY BIRD

A flicker
A flutter
Suddenly you arrive
Perched within this berry bush
Where
For a magic moment
You remain
Pert and poised
And very still
Your lovely little head cocked
And tiny eye
Fixed on me

I am still
Transfixed
But then
So quickly I can't imagine how
You are on another limb
Busy picking something tasty
I suppose
From your host's bare branch
Or nearby leaf

Then
In an inkling
You move on and
With a flicker
And a flutter
You are gone

Tiny guest
Your brief visit
Was a quick brush stroke
Of bright beauty
On the canvas of
My day

Though for one brief moment
Your lovely image I beheld
I shall remember
And be glad

For this
Your unexpected gift
I am grateful
Tiny little bird
To you and
To the one who sent you
And so can only say
Do come again!

WIDE PRAIRIE

Long
So long the flat horizon
As though
God
With a cosmic rule in hand
Had drawn
And spread it so

Above
Along the long plain's edge
A drifting cloud
Spreads lacy arms
As if to bless or
Caress
The prairie land
Below

Blazing sun
Warms the wind
That bends the prairie grass
While cattle gather at a
Lonely windmill tank
And bury eager noses
In the earth's
Cool water

WIDE WORLD

Wide
So wide the world
Ringing with a mystic
Symphony
A harmony of love and wonder
Joy and
Pain

You birthed me
Raised
Called
Opened and enthralled me
And bound me
With a mortal chain

Now
Enamored and
Entrapped
I drink deep of
Vistas
Vast and grand
Far rolling seas and fronded isles
Wind swept beaches where
Calling gulls
Glide over snow white sand

Tall rise your
Ancient mountains
Robed deep in fragrant pine
Dark shadowed and alive

Where
Safe within your verdant bosom
Dwell your children
Of another kind

So wide indeed
This ancient world
Where a million million souls
Through the sweep of
Countless ages
Dream and build
Love
Hate
And destroy
Then
Build again
And at last
Move on

Move on
Yet leave in passing
A wide, wide world
Brim full to
Overflowing
Resounding with a song
Unheard
Unsung
The anthem of creation
We give the name of
God

Section 2

Along The Way

A DRIVE TO CHURCH

It has become our habit
For my good wife and me
To drive to church
Each Sunday
Fresh scrubbed
And In our Sabbath best
All quite proper
And ready
To be blest

Now I will admit
As we drive and
Strollers amble by
Or customers at Starbucks
Settle back in ease
I sigh

For there comes a bit of envy
I will not pretend
For God must surely be as near
To those who walk
The dappled path
Or sip a Sunday latte
With a friend

For God is everywhere
I've been taught
In church or out
Along the wayward path
Where some may sense
The holy Presence
While others
Perhaps not

Where some may say
A prayer or two
And others give it
Scarce a thought

So we drive to church
Our Sunday habit
Don't you know
Where we will find
Our God alive in others
As once they did in Jesus
Long ago

Here all together
Faith assembled
Vision once more clarified
Strength renewed and
With holy comfort blest
We will be thankful
For our Sunday habit
As we drive to church
To give the One who is
Truly everywhere
Our Sunday best

A WORD OR TWO

A word
Or two
Of angels or of
Lesser folk
May do the work of demons
Or of saints
To open channels of
Divine redemption and
Build foundations for
A nation's prosperity and hope
For all its blend of souls

It appears ironic and almost
Obscene that
From so small and fallible a source
Such a potent stream may start
Giving evidence of beginning
In a human brain
Or heart

And it must surely follow
That wherever
Inspiration or direction issues from
Such mortal declaration
And action follows
In measure great or small
Kings and common folk alike
May walk a different path
Tomorrow

Surely such an observation
This admonition must suggest
To carefully consider
Where our Words are used
And when

Be they by folks like us
Or those in highest station
Who the rudder of the
Ship of State may tend
Or it may be
Only pass an hour or two
Sharing gossip with a friend

Thus this thought remains to
Ponder
That a simple word may curse
Or bless our way
And even human fate decide
While in a less fraught moment
Friends in passing
May simply share
The time of day

So in this matter it seems
A danger lurks in
All our speaking
Since with words
Untimely sent
It seems quite possible
To insert a foot
Into a careless mouth
And find
Alas
That words are useless and
There's nothing left to do
But simply to
Repent!

AUDACITY

I suppose it may appear
Audacious
To ever question God
Tho' Job as I recall
Got away with doing it
And raised a question
About his fate
That seemed quite in order
After all

Now in the face of what may seem
Our human misadventure
It may appear it's time again
To query the Almighty
To ask if after all
We're headed for
Disaster

Now to be sure
The records show
We've been this way before
When mankind's always
Shaky roof has
Nearly tumbled in
With nasty wars
Or nature's crush
And no small assist
From human sin

Yet somehow
As the ages pass
All cataclysms have an end
Storm clouds break
And flee away
While they who once were
Counted foe
Are now embraced as friend

Is the question then
Audacious
Does our impatience
Fault the quest
Is God's unseen hand
Still working
In this troubled world's affairs
Do the ways of the Eternal
Yet unfold across the ages
Showing that Eternal Love
Still cares?

So we must trust
As once did Job
That even in life's stormy gale
We are in the
Hand of a caring God
Whose Eternal Love
Will in time
Prevail

AN ORDINARY DAY

Is there
If the truth be told
Such a thing
As just
An ordinary day?
For
After all
Each measures
One more step along
The way
Each is given
Although
The final sum
Remains
Unknown

But then
I shall not worry
Nor fret
But rather be about
Those very ordinary things
I have not done
Just yet!

The adventure
After all
Is for the up and doing
Whatever may be be asked
With such gifts
As have been given
Whatever the task

For there are paths
We've never known before
And still others
Though once we trod
Waiting to be trod
Once more

So may this day become
A new and grand adventure
Though no mountain climbed
Or rushing river crossed
Let us yet rejoice that
We've been blest
With yet another
Ordinary day
Before
At last
We rest

BELOVED INTERLUDE

So small a thing
Though greater things are often less
I'm sure
But to be your companion for
The next few miles or more
To sing a song or two
And laugh like crazy
Or cry
As may be fitting

To paint the airy walls in flowers
Or dancing dragons
Or paper them with solemn plans
Whose time may someday come
Although
Perhaps
Something better will intervene
Explode in bright surprise
And you and I
Will laugh or cry
Tomorrow

COMPLEXITY AND HOPE

Ah yes
A word quite fit for
Verbal mastication
To chew upon and
Ponder long
Its choice a
Predilection

For certainly it seems
To fit quite well
The scene we often encounter
Life's bits and pieces all askew
Where nothing seems to matter

But stubborn hope springs anew
Though all appear in tatters
We will find an order soon
And a sign
That chaos
Matters!

Then shall this complexity
That now seems so confusing
Align itself at last to hope
And a future
Much more
Promising

CERTAINTY

Are you certain?
Asked a curious friend
Who found my affirmation
Quite enough to raise the brows
Of those of
Alternate persuasion

But my reply was not
Such as ends discussion
But often brings a fervent
Counterpoint

For certainty
Is after all a state of mind
Resulting from gathering
Things long observed
Experienced
Read in many books
Or gleaned from other minds
And conversations

All of which indeed may lead
To personal convictions
Held in sincere passion
Or with a milder frame of mind

For in light of ages past
All of us should understand
That our most ardent affirmations

Tomorrow may be challenged
Altered or replaced
By what then proves to be
A better or perhaps wiser
Point of view

DEVOTION

A head bowed down is
Not required
Though it may suggest
A humble and a contrite spirit
Or an attitude of prayer

But devotion follows many paths
When directed by the
Mind or heart
And points the life in directions
Not always visioned at the start

True devotion does not require
Confession or contrition
But depending on occasion or
The object of its quest
May signify a certain state
Of mind or purpose
Evidence of commitment to
A goal envisioned
As the best

But when romance brightens
The horizon
And life is filled with
Hearts and flowers
Romance blossoms like a million poppies
On a springtime hillside
After April showers

Then, as the rolling seasons pass
Life slows its frantic pace
Devotion deepens and matures
Painting the glowing western sky
With the brush of
Love long cherished
And devotion bows a grateful head
In prayer

DUTY

Why should the word
Sound stuffy
Or maybe even
Stiff
When it defines what
Every life embraces
Or by Duty's servants is
Often embraced?

When our path is graced by
Unearned mercy
Or blest with some
Unexpected gift
Then
With spirit humbled
And our heart
Fresh warmed
We are taught
That life suggests some
Recompense is due
Or perhaps our
Gratitude implies response in kind
A moral echo it may be
To keep the scale
In balance

And so
Although duty
Surely would not be
The word
To suit the obligation
It is surely not amiss
To do what one's own
Heart suggests
Whatever word
Describes it
Best

EVER LEARNING

One learns
With passing years
You cannot always be
So sure
Things once taken
To be true
Are really all one thought
Though once emblazoned
As a maxim
"This I know"

For life and circumstance
Have their way
Of molding the most
Orthodox
To see complexity
And shades of grey
Almost everywhere

Thus does one come
At last to understand
That sacred myth and fable
Have ever been
The medium and the vessel
Of the Spirit's message
And its power
With faith
Hope
And love
The most powerful
Of all

FAITH OF A LATTER DAY

I'm no longer
Quite so sure
Of all I once believed
Or thought I knew
Life has its way
And provides its own
Higher education
Teaching this today
And that tomorrow
Undoing lessons learned
Just yesterday

Yes, I know
The elders taught
What older elders
Believed they knew
And it seems
Lived virtuous lives
Behind close-shuttered minds

And I suppose
That was best for them
In their time and place
And they were blest and happy
Within those stern limits
That now seem strangely quaint
Or perhaps
Sometimes improper

All the same
The lessons they once taught
So long ago
Underlying all the rest
And coming home on this
My latter day
Seems altogether plain

Be humble in
The face of life
And its sometime
Confusing lessons
The only certainty
Among the clamor of the creeds
Is this
Love is ever best
God is kind
And we do not walk alone
Among the stars

FROM WHERE I SIT

From where I sit
Just now
Observing the world of
Things around
All seems rather mundane
Ordinary
In a comfortable sort of way

But of course
That could be deceptive
For beyond these mundane moments
I am aware
A world in turmoil
Twists and turns
Where millions trudge a
Perilous path
Along the edge of death
Dreaming of a crust of bread
Or a cup of cool water

Yet
While I sit pondering
The might of great nations
Debate of guns, arms and treaties
And trade deals worth
Many million euros, yen or dollars

While one, small crumpled bill
Given from a caring hand
Would feed a hungry mouth
And bring a flicker of hope
In the pleading eyes
Of the ragged soul that sits
Waiting at the corner of nowhere
Yet everywhere
For someone very much like me
To care

GROWING TO BE WISE

They say we use but
One small part
Of the brain that we've
Been given
And using what we have
May stimulate a scholarly
Ambition

Books then become
Our stepping stones
To becoming more informed
Perhaps to earning an
Advanced degree
With a PhD adorned

Yet there's a virtue
Study lends
Both in and out of books
The open and thirsty mind
Contemplates and studies
All it sees
At everything it looks

So to wisely live and prosper
Is to study and expand
To enlarge the mind and
Grow the heart
Until at last
We understand

That life best lived
Is life flung open
To lessons
From whatever source
So may we bless the earth
In passing
On this fascinating planet
We call home

INSPIRATION

When starting out to
Write a word
Or two
To awaken it may be
A slumbering imagination
One often seeks the aid of
Some extraordinary muse
To provide a touch of
Holy inspiration

Yet Providence
It appears
Is averse to vain ambition
And often deigns to bless
The ordinary and plain
With profound
And what may be
Redeeming revelation

For he who once
Upon a far-off rocky shore
Spoke while those about him
Mended nets
Talked of ordinary things
Within the lives of
Humble folk he knew
Their hopes and dreams
And God's love for everyone
Folks just like me
And you

So as I seek a fitting phrase
To satisfy a critic's ear
I must remember him
Who once taught
Beside the Galilean shore
And whose plain and
Kindly words
Still echo down
The marching years

IS AND WAS

I am an IS
And of course that means
I WAS
And you must be as well
For if you
Or I
Should only be a WAS
Then our time of IS
Could only mean ONCE WAS
And I would not be writing
As I am
Nor you reading or hearing
As you are
Patiently or not

For WAS-NESS means
Our time of being IS over
Past and done
And we are history
After all
Though perhaps
Written rather small

Yet I am glad today
To celebrate a modest
IS-NESS
Until that time
Shall come
When It shall be said of me
He WAS...

JUST FOR FUN

O hum diddle dee
Or perhaps diddle diddle
I'll write you a rhyme
Or maybe a riddle
But seeing at riddles I'm
Not very clever
I'll opt for the rhyme
A more hopeful endeavor!

I'm not serious of course
I've been serious for eons
But now just for fun
For both prophets and peons
I'm penning this verse
O diddle dee dee
Of poetic nonsense
And do it for free!

So hi diddie diddie
Ho hum diddle do
Let's toast to the moon
And toast to you too

Now let's all join hands
As they strike up the band
And dance in a circle
So give me your hand

Let's laugh and be giddy
Clap hands while relaxing
And do nothing at all
That's overly taxing

So join hands and circle
Dance 'round in a ring
They're fixing a banquet
That's fit for a king

But the king has absconded
Well so much for that
And the queen has gone shopping
To buy a new hat

So la la boola boola
Or perhaps boola boo
Hooray for the lady who
Lived in a shoe
Her children were many
They drove her berserk
So many offspring
Was just too much work!

She retired with a pension
For telling her story
She's now living in heaven
And resting in glory

So dance 'round rejoicing
Let's have a great time
But when the music stops playing
We'll all stop
On
A
Dime!

LIGHT AND SHADOWS

We seek the light
Are drawn
As moths to candle flame
Though we perhaps
To some less lethal brightness

All the same
We too are moved to seek
Whatever light we find
That may best illumine
Our often benighted lives
Or perhaps
Enhance
This many-shadowed world

But we shall not escape
The shadows
Nor fail to find them
For they too belong
As counterpoint and balance
Of the whole
Giving definition
To what it is
We cherish most
Though ever
Accented
By what we may
Least desire
In the shadows

MY PEACE

Tonight
The sky is clear
Or nearly so
For there are clouds
Drifting like great ghosts
Across the face of
Moon and stars

So it seems
Life has days
When skies are clear
Where all seems plain
Everything in place
Though inevitably
One must deal with
A cloud or two

For I have learned
Long since
Not to feign omnipotence
But rather to accept
The limits of an
Ever more obvious
Mortality

Thus gladly do I leave questions
That are too large for me
To others
And to God
And in this assurance
Find at last
My peace

NO BREAD

The ceiling fan whirs on
Almost silently
The moving air breathes
'Round my face
Cooler now
And I am grateful

But surely my gratitude must be
Broader far than that
A more pressing obligation
For more than pleasant
Circulation

When a moment's brief reflection
Recalls the sorry plight of
Millions
Fleeing hopelessness and death
Chance a grim voyage across
Wild, uncertain seas
Only to find
On touching shore in
More favored lands
Hear the words, "Move On!"

My chair is comfortable
And I wonder about dinner
It's nearly time
The wine is airing in the kitchen
And my wife will say
"It's ready" soon

But what of those
The unseen homeless
Fleeing with crying child
And there is
No bread?

"Hurry, it will get cold" she calls
And I rise to seat myself
At a table
Modestly laden with what an
Incredible privilege provides

Yes, we will say "grace"
Trusting a kindly Providence knows
Our sincere if modest gratitude
While we wonder
All the same
Even as I lift my fork
What will become of those
Who flee the terror
And they have
No bread

OF BRAWN AND BRAIN

He was big
And tall
Six feet five or more
Of solid muscle and bone that
Made him proud
So he could take on
Anyone at all
Or so he said
And few would dare
To disagree

But it gives one pause
When weighty issues rise
As such issues often do
And wiser minds suggest
To sit awhile and give it thought
To find the way
That may prove to be
The best

A bulging bicep
Or an iron fist
Give little aid to a troubled nation
Or offer a solution
To a farmer
Whose fields are brown and bare
And whose well
Is dry

So it clearly appears
That might is more than muscle
And aptitudes of mind and heart
More truly define a worthy soul
And provide the promise
Of a better world tomorrow
Where love and justice play
The truly greater part

OH MY

Oh my!
Say I
When first I gaze
Upon a tasty crumpet
Topped with frosting
Don't you know
And I truly long
And ardently desire
To have it

Ah, but then
I do recall
My sincere determination
To lose a pound or two
This week
That would cause my wife
Elation

But with coffee hot and black
It would seem to me
A crime
Not to add a bite or two
And make this pause
Sublime

So I stand and ponder long
This gastronomic sinning
Anticipating pounds of course
And not much hope of thinning
So now I slowly turn away
To consume a luncheon salad
A victory of sorts
Perhaps
To conclude this
Woeful ballad

PROCRASTINATION

Wait
Yes I know
It needs doing
And it should be done
Without a doubt
Right now

Yet
As I consider
And feel a nag inside
Still I'm aware that urgency
Is relative
And there may be a little space
Between this very moment and
When I really must
Decide

Yes I know
Why not just do it now?
Wouldn't it be best
If it were a task completed
And off that nagging list?

Of course
Such cogent observation
Is plain to see
But there remains this prospect
Of another lovely moment's rest
Until at last
Accompanied by a sigh
I will really up and do it
By and by

REALITY

We know reality
Of course we do
Our common sense tells us so
Just take my hand
Or listen to the gentle wind
Gaze upon the rolling hills
Or touch the soft, new fallen snow

But then we're told
By those who
More thoroughly explore
That all we thought
We knew
Is not really what we
Thought it was before

For all it seems consists
Of a billion billion particles
In motion
Arranged by cosmic evolution in
Countless intricate designs
To be
For you and me
What certainly appears to be
A quite solid and substantial
Reality

Of course
There are the years gone by
And what went on back then
The reality of yesteryear

Preserved in countless dusty books
By many an ancient pen

But now the scholars
Have disclosed
That bygone years were
Not always quite the same
As ancient tale
And treasured myth supposed

Reality
We are told
In history as in countless
Other things
Wears more the look of
Common days
Bearing witness to the work
Of common folk
And the changes hard work brings

But certainly there's now and then
A great one
Large or small
To put a finger on the scale
And shape and change
Both life and times for all
Turning history at last to myth
In many a glorious book

So lives are touched and noble
Dreams are born

With great kingdoms built and
Battles won
Thus is history forever changed
By reality turned myth
To become at last a
Redeeming tale
To bring all life at last to God
On a truly transformed earth

SOMETIMES

Sometimes
Like
Now
When all the items
On my list of things to do
Are done
Almost
Though this or that might
Require a tidy up
Or two
I pause to take a breath
Though my body
Not require it
My mind says
Whoa!

It's then
I sometimes ponder
Just a bit
About tomorrow
Not just beyond this sunset
But beyond them all

That last sunset will come
Sometime
When all the items on
My list of things to do are done
Or might have been
Tho' they never made the list

That someday sometime
Will be a time to ponder
And reflect
About what mattered after all
When all our times and sometimes
Have reached their end

Ah but then
On that glorious someday
As that splendid morning breaks
My sometime will become
Forever
And my last someday
Will become
A blessed eternity
With God

STILL WONDERING

Just got to wondering a bit
About the shape
This old world
Is in
And if tomorrow
Or a year or two
Might find human fortunes
Rather thin

For if our errant race
Declines to pay attention
While glaciers melt away
And oceans rise
Will millions raise their hands
In much belated prayers
Expecting their redemption
From dark
Polluted skies?

Wisdom yet cries out
From hearts and minds aware
That destiny is shaped
By souls awake
With busy hands
That have learned
To care

For if God is in the details
And all of this is planned
Then deity is in those hearts
That seek to understand
That destiny is home grown stuff
And fate the choice we ponder
And we had best be busy
There's no time left
To squander

Yet
When all decisions
Have been made
All actions planned are taken
'Tis love alone will matter most
And humankind awaken!

THE QUESTION

He looked me in the eye
And asked
Are you saved?
Yes, was my reply
Since many years ago I gave
All the heart I had
To all the God I knew
Trusting Jesus
As indeed
I still do

Yet now
The years have passed
And I wonder
Is it quite so simple
As it seemed back then
For questions rise
And beg for answers
Demanded
By an every-searching mind

Saved from what
To What
And what sort of God
Condemns the sincere and
Just believer
Of some other faith than mine
Though his lamp of life
Shines brighter than my own

For there must be
A million, million souls
Who never heard the Name
Or if they did
It seemed an idle tale
However beautiful
So they remained
True to what was taught them
From their fathers long ago
Echoing the ages

So it appears
I must revise
My perspective
To acknowledge other paths
Than just my own
Remaining very glad
That Jesus came
And shed new light upon
The way
Saving me for Heaven
And so much more

For "saved"
I've found
Is fully living for today
And all days to be
Standing tall for all that's
Just and right

Loving both my friend
My foe
As did my Master
Long ago

So now I dare believe
I am embraced
With all God's children
Of every clan or calling
Bid by his spirit
Deep within
To hold out a loving hand
And open wide my heart
To all who share this
Wide earth with me
'till Heaven bids
A welcome Home

THE TRUTH

Is it true
What you just said?
Would you believe it
Had it come from me?

But yes
As winds that blow from
East or west
Are indeed the same
Though born in varied climes
They yet may carry
In an airy bosom
Leaves from many trees

So does truth
Often appear in different guise
Since from different voices
It is often heard
Carrying with it from
Some other mind's direction
A different point of view

Thus to know the truth
In matter large or small
It would be best
To hold it up and turn it 'round
In many different lights
So may it appear in all
Its possible dimensions
And all contention find
At last
A peaceful
Resolution

THE UNKNOWN

Like a furtive knock
Upon an unopened door
To write a word or more
About the vast unknown
Seems destined to be
An exercise in fantasy
Or describe an
Empty space

Yet
That seductive emptiness still
Mystifies
Still draws the mind to
Ponder and explore
To imagine and to dream
Using tools at hand
To construct upon the
Blank page of tomorrow
What the mind or
Perhaps the heart may
Dare suggest

The stuff of fantasy you say?
And no doubt it is true
So surely care must be taken
To respect some sensible
Parameters after all

Although
The world we find so real today
Is filled with much
That yesterday could scarcely
Dare imagine
And those who daily knock upon

The tantalizing door of
The vast unknown
May yet enter and explore
A world we may someday
Openly embrace
And shaking heads may say
"Why didn't we think of
That before?"

THEOLOGY

Thinking
About God
Can leave one's head
Spinning
Tho' of course
Many brave that
Cerebral vertigo
In hope of learning
Who or what
Or where
Or how
God is

Yet
I am convinced
The effort's worth
The spin
And that
It's no sin
To seek to understand
What we mean
When we say
"God"

THY KINGDOM COME

We pray the words
Each Sunday
When time comes 'round
Rote, no doubt
Though none the less sincere
For fear perhaps
If we did not
Something might slip
In the vast
Eternal plan

Yet I surmise
On more profound reflection
That if God be God
The Kingdom will come
In His good time
Even should my praying slip
A cog or two
The White Sox win the Pennant
Or the infield grass turn blue

Yet still I pray
"Thy Kingdom come"

Even if it should only be
In me
For I gladly surrender
Jurisdiction
Wherever it is mine
Trusting that in
The progress of creeping ages
All the rest of
God's eternal plan
Will at last
On earth
Be done

TO AWAKEN

Just got to wondering a bit
About the shape
This old world
Is in
And if tomorrow
Or a year or two
Might find human fortunes
Rather thin

For if our errant race
Declines to pay attention
While glaciers melt
And oceans rise
Will millions raise their hands
In much belated prayers
Expecting their redemption
From dark
Polluted skies

Wisdom yet cries out
From hearts and minds aware
That destiny is shaped
By souls awake
With busy hands
That have learned
To care

For if God is in the details
And all is planned
Then deity is in those hearts
That seek to understand
That destiny is home grown stuff
And fate the choice we ponder
And we had best be busy
There's no time left
To squander

Yet
When all decisions
Have been made
All actions planned are taken
'Tis love alone will matter most
And humankind awaken

TO BE PERFECTLY PRACTICAL

It's probably not possible
To be perfectly practical
About anything at all
Although
Many an earnest soul it seems
Makes a daily task
Or pilgrimage may be
To shape the world as close
To that elusive ideal
As human skill
Or devout diligence may allow

Undeterred
Disdaining the frailty of mortal flesh
Or the occasional cloud that
Drifts across the inner sky
Of every dreamer or pilgrim
Of our common way
Or perhaps it should be
We
Press on!

Yet we are clearly in their debt
Who plod a lesser path
And settle for a goal
Within this world of stubborn
Imperfection
"I've fixed it!
Not perfect but
It works"
Yet we must honor those pioneers
Of an illusive grand dimension
For they often lift our common life
Above where it would ever be
Without them

TODAY

We sometimes act
As if today
Was a time apart
Disconnected from all other
Days and times
By an unseen wall
As though what happened
"Way back then"
Doesn't really matter any more
Or is
Inconsequential
In the drama of a vigorous
Today

Yet
Such a disconnect is clearly
A wishful dream
For the very stuff
Today is made of
In reality
Is but the residue of
All our yesterdays
Passed on through time's
Swift revolving door
It becomes
The building blocks
Which you and I
May assemble for today
Opening the way
To construct a more just
And beautiful
Tomorrow

TWO WORLDS

The drive is not so long
From where I live
To go downtown
A freeway and an avenue
Beneath an overpass
A bridge or two
With a signal now and then
And perhaps a bit of
Irritation
We are at last
Downtown

Yet it's disconcerting on the way
To view the changes wrought
Upon the sprawling city's face
By the countless homeless folk
Who call this vast metropolis
Their home

From million dollar mansions
On favored streets and
Hills nearby
To makeshift tents beneath the
Bridges and overpass
Where a ragged sleeper lies curled
Against a graffiti covered wall
Two worlds lie painfully in view
Oblivious to those who pass
Trying not to see

What can we do
Who profess to love and care
To mend the shattered bonds
And create a new and human city
Of the cluttered contradiction
That is this sprawling place?

Indeed
We often pray
And seek what appears to be
A most elusive inspiration
Though now
As we drive swiftly by
Two worlds remain
For those with eyes to see
One beneath bridges and
Overpass
The other on the city's verdant
Streets and hills
And both within our
Burdened hearts

And so our fervent prayer remains:
Dear God, it surely must not be!
Show us the path
And with it
Hearts and eyes to
More clearly see.

WHEN CHILDREN DIE

When children die
Be they others' or
Our own
The heart is numb with grief
And in desperation cries
"Dear God
Why?"

Yet
Upon reflection it
Is plain
That mortality embraces
All alike
And accident or illness
Do not always pay
The calendar
Or our affections
The attention we
So ardently
Desire

"But where was God?"
We ask
"Who Jesus taught us loves
The little children
And in his arms
Reached out
To hold them close?"

Close by
And no doubt was
Weeping too
For greater love can
Only greater grieve
When the hands of
Circumstance or fate

Deal a heartbreak
To those to whom this
Earth is given
With all its possibility
For love
And hope
And danger too

No
God is not far away
When children die
When dreams are crushed
And the breaking heart
Cries out
"Why?"

For he who suffered Calvary
And himself once gave
That anguished cry
Was not left dying there alone
Without his God
But in the Easter sunrise
As today in countless hearts and
Grateful lives
The risen Christ lives on
To hold all earth's children
Close

WHERE GOD IS

I've wondered
Haven't you?
Why God hides
Behind the sky
Invisible
To my searching eye

But perhaps
God is not invisible
At all
But smiling
From each lovely
Ordinary thing

And I
If only I would
Look within
Would find God
Speaking still
In my native tongue

For it seems
We're much inclined
To seek for God
In some "other" place
Yet all the while
God is
Quite close by
In ordinary things

WORDS

Words, words, words!
Come pouring by the billion
From countless mouths
And computers by the score
Though now and then
In some patient hand
A pen

A difference in this troubled world?
Some sorely needed change?
Some new direction for our
Struggling human race?
Or just a surplus of emotion
Or perhaps exasperation
At so leisurely a pace

Still
It is our way
Communicating daily
The most serious things
We believe we know
For all our progress
Our hopes
And plans
Depend on joint endeavor
And surely we must act together
Or that dreamed of
Bright tomorrow
May instead be
Never

We do depend on
Articulated dreams
Or plans passed on
And shared with others who
Can make tomorrow
Somehow better
Than that which was
Just yesterday
Seen to be
The best

So Words
For all their
Generous supply
And while a nuisance
They may often seem
Remain the indispensable bridge
For our most human meanings
To cross between
And provide
For unity
And peace
So we may unite
And together build
And fulfill
The human dream

WINE
(An abbreviated history)

How many eons
Must have gone by
Since first some ancient
Humanoid
First noted that
The wrinkled grapes he
Crushed into his mouth
Were different
And quite pleasant
After all
And so he had
Some more

Thus it began
And step by juicy step
Our ancestors learned to
Pick and press and
Then to age awhile
This gift that nature
And the vine
Bestowed
Until today
It sits before me as
My lovely glass
Of wine

Section 3

Seasons

A CHRISTMAS WORLD

Dare we dream
Of a Christmas world
Though centuries have passed
Since first that gleaming star
Shone down

Still
From Mary's babe
Grown tall
A brighter light has shone
Than a million stars could muster
Or that one star alone

Yes
There are lights
Of other kinds
In other lands we know
And other voices
Call out to all
And point their lives
To God

Still
The Christmas star shines brightly
In every year and time
And finds its glow reflected
Throughout all lands and climes

Could it be then after all
A day
Or night may be
When there shall be
A Christmas world
For all to see

For
The light of love
Illumines all
Who open wide their heart
And Mary's babe
Even yet is born
Whenever love is known

ADVENT ALWAYS

Once again
The Season dawns
This time of holy
Preparation
Giving birth once more
To long-held dreams
Whose ancient roots go deep
In our own
And many nations

It was his birth
Though inauspicious
At the time
That marked the dawn of
A gentle revolution
In dusty Galilee
And far beyond
Sparked by the carpenter
Turned preacher
That this babe became
But then he died
Crucified

It was they said
For challenging the cruel status quo
That government and Temple
Had so clearly specified

But neither grizzly gallows
Nor borrowed tomb
Could dim the hope he'd sown
Or quench the love
The common folk had found
When at his bidding
They opened hearts and arms
To form a holy and redeeming bond

At last
Multiplied a million times and more
This love became a
Blest contagion
That turned an empire upside down
And spread at last
To every nation

So now
As Advent once again
Celebrates his coming
May we not forget the
Path he trod
Or neglect to follow
The way he opened
Home at last
To God

CANDLEMAS

Blessed be the Light
Tiny though its flame appear
Against the vastness
Of the surrounding dark

Insignificant may seem
This bit of wax
This minuscule wick
And the tiny flame
That dances and weaves
Atop its candle host

Still
As the flame
Portending a brighter light
By far
Casts its glow
Against the shadowed bastions
Of the night
So shall at last
That Greater Light
Illumine all the
Darkened places of the earth

For he who was the Light
Has ignited
A worldwide conflagration
So that now
A million candles
Glow where once was One

Then let this blessed candle
Of the Candlemas
Portray to all
His body in the wax
His soul the wick
His Spirit bright the flame

Illumined by this holy fire
Let us rejoice
As in our fleeting day
We join
The irresistible dawning
Of His wondrous
And redeeming Light!

HOLY DAYS

Holy days and
Sacred seasons
Come on silent feet into
Our often pell-mell world of
Work and worry
Fuss and strain
Bringing a welcome note of
Wonder, joy and love
To harried souls
Giving each a chance to pause
And to touch once more
The blessed hem
Of peace

So does the Christmas star
Send its sacramental gleam
Down the path of
Ever-succeeding years
Forever to shine bright welcome
To the sacred birth
It still leads earth's
Wisest pilgrims
To behold

For he became a pilgrim too
This peasant preacher
Healer, kindly friend
Walking dusty paths and
Gathering his peasant crowd
To sit beneath an ancient sycamore

To hear in simple rhyme and story
Of God's love for the least and lost
And all humble souls who
Open hungry hearts to each other
And to God

He died
A martyr's death
Betrayed by a friend and
Crucified
And yet
He lives
Beyond the threat of mortal power
Or danger now
He lives forever
In hearts like those of ones
Who heard beneath the
Ancient sycamore
The voice of him who died
And is alive forever
The one whose love
And justice
Lives still in those who follow
Not just in
Sacred seasons or on Holy days
But on every day
And will
Someday
Rule the world

JESUS OF NAZARETH

He was a babe
Peasant born
Of lowly birth
And plain
Rome ruled
The world he knew
Hard fisted
Sword in hand

But he grew
Became a man
Strong willed
Yet tempered
With loving heart
And soul
Close-knit
To God

He healed the sick
And walked
On humble paths to
Dusty hamlets
Among the peasant folk
He loved and taught
Cast their demons out
Ate their common bread
And drank
Their peasant wine

Until at last
He drew a throng
And took his cause
To Jerusalem
The Temple
And in the face
Of Rome

He died
Crucified
As those who dare
Oppose the tyrant's sword
Yet it's told
By those who loved him best
He rose!

So now
He lives
Among us yet
And his spirit yet recruits
A kindly army
Filled with passion
For his God

So shall the victory be
His at last
All swords laid down
All spears aside
And love shall rule
The world

LABOR DAY

Sitting here in
My weathered chair
I remember
As the calendar declares
That this leisure has
A title after all
And my serenity is not
Nameless as my repose
May make it seem
As it was long since christened
Labor Day

So I suppose
Sitting here in easy
Contemplation
I celebrate for this aging
Flesh and bone
A lack of labor
Truth be told
It is a gift, you know
Of growing old!

Others no doubt don't find it
Quite this way
For my good wife
Even now
Attends to our collected washing
With ironing to follow
Later in the day

Trader Joe's just down the street
Has doors wide open
Even this Labor Day
Clerks and staff are busy too
With cheery smiles and busy hands
And of course
A healthy check in view

And I surmise
While pondering it all
That great corporations
Even on this anointed Day
Do not pause
Or even stall
For it's just
Another day to make money
After all
Which is their way

But as for me
I shall still
My blissful ease enjoy
Celebrating Labor Day in
Rest and relaxation
For work and rest both
Have their place
Across this busy world of ours
And in every land
And nation

TO MY VALENTINE

Stalwart doesn't sound romantic
Or conjure roses by the score
But for you my constant love
It says so much...and more!

Your beloved presence every day
Tending to our needs or wishes
All I can do is write this poem
And then of course
I can at least
Dry the dishes!

But there's so much more
Though words a-plenty would be wasted
All that is needed I am sure
Is a candle lighted dinner
Just for us two
That may be tasted

So when current maladies subside
And busy schedules resume
Let's plan to celebrate this blessed bond
With dinner at the lovely Langham
Of which both of us are
Very fond

So my beloved stalwart wife
I do salute you on this day
But I am running out of words
Though there is so
Much more I could say

In sincere love and great appreciation

Section 4

Remembering

"BABE"

Alexander Howard Grant
His parents named him finally
But this younger son
Took an early name
And remained to the family
"Uncle Babe"

He never married
Though he courted now and then
And he was a handsome man
This tall, Scots-Irish man
Yet his aging mother needed him
And maybe that is why
Though who can say for sure

And it doesn't matter now
Uncle Babe is gone
But he leaves a legacy
Memories sown soul-deep
In all the kin
The children he loved
And cherished as his own
Since he loved them so
They were his children too

He never had a house
To call his own
He never made a fortune
Or a name
But lived with the others
Who had their places
And welcomed him in
As part of the family

He could be gruff
And was at times
A stern reminder of a day
When life was not so easy
And a man learned to work
And save
"Turn out the lights
When you leave the room"
Babe often said
Yes
We'll remember

But he loved to laugh
And fish
And as the years came on
He seemed to grow somehow
More alive
At peace perhaps with what
Life brought or failed to bring
And as his generation left him
One by one
He filled well the place he held
As kindly patriarch of a
Passing clan

And at last
As time slowed his steps
He seemed to know
It would not be very long
And gladly passed what he
Had worked so hard to save
To younger hands
Some less careful than his own

He has gone
But Heaven must be joyful
As beloved family gathers there
To welcome Alexander home
And the Master leads him to
His own place at last
Reserved for one
Who graced the world
With the sort of
Kind and staunch humanity
That was our
"Uncle Babe"

BENEATH THE SURFACE

Sometimes
When a tranquil calm
Presides upon life's
Inward ocean
One may be tempted
To believe
That all the storms and turmoil
Of the soul
Have found at last
A peaceable
Conclusion

Ah, but then
The day does inevitably arrive
When inner weather once more
Alters
When fresh winds of question
Or doubt arise
And confidence in long held
Certainties of the soul
To our dismay
May falter

Yet wisdom teaches
That this storm
As those before
Will pass
And in its ending leave
A gift of wisdom
And of holy patience
Until the schooling of all our
Mortal years
Is past

BRAND PARK
(Glendale, CA)

What brand of Park is Brand?
She asked
(or words to that effect)
I said I really didn't know
Because
I hadn't been there yet

And so we went
And walked the grass
And prowled here and there
Exploring up the canyon too
(They didn't seem to care)
The library was interesting
Though slim on dance and stuff
But books and records by the score
(Really quite enough)
We poked and prowled a little more
And then returned delighted
For Brand was a delightful brand
That
We both
Decided

A FOND MEMORY OF BROTHER ROD

Roderick Nay Grant
So he was named at birth
My brother had arrived
My world but two years old
Now enlarged by one

We grew
And one year later Bruce arrived
Marian following but
A few years more
So now we were four
The "Grant kids" thrived!

We tussled, Rod and I
As brothers will
Mind and body too
My edge the latter
His the former for
Early on
It appeared
He would prosper
In academia and more
Which he did quite well
With victories and records
On the track
Before
It was "off to Cal"
A University
And then
The world

World War Two
Swallowed up a year or two
For both Rod and me until
At warfare's end
We went our separate ways

Off to school again
And then
Brother Rod went to work for
Uncle Sam
And assignment overseas

Now with wife Marianne
A son was born
And after Kenneth
Laurie too
And the Grant Clan grew

Years in Paris at a
State Department desk
And not even a
Terrorist bomb's near miss
Deterred him from his work

So on to Germany, Bonn
And later still Taipei
Until home at last in USA
A crazed intruder with a gun
Came too close and left a scar
But brother Rod lived on

Retired at last
In pleasant West Coast Washington
And later still to Ashburn VA
He turned to writing
Poetry

Brother Roderick left his mark
In State Department annals
And certainly far more
Writing poignant lines that
Would someday find print
And penned
Five books in all
Before
At eighty eight
He died

So much of Roderick Grant
Lives on in all he wrote
His wide-ranging mind revealed
His heart disclosed
A wealth of poignant thought
Unfolding line by line
To tell the world
He left behind
Here was a good
And thoughtful man
Who surely left this world
Better and far richer
Than he found it.

By a grateful brother, Ken

DEAR FRIEND

Are we not a family dear friend?
Though not linked beneath the skin
By blood
It really doesn't matter after all
The "ties that bind" are deeper than
What courses through our veins
And the spirit that warms us in
Our time together
Has a certain holy air
Suggesting that the Source is
Heart inhaled
And near at hand

Friends so close are bonded
After all
Though no solemn words are said
To sanctify the tie
A marriage has transpired
Where souls have found a melding
In the rush and tumble
Of a common day

So let us celebrate, dear friend,
And be grateful that we've found
The unexpected
But really delightful gift of
This nameless bond
That in a world of lonely hearts
Is simply called
A friend

"GEORGE MONTY"

Resplendent
Proud and slowly strutting
Before an awestruck crowd
Silently
Beholding with curious gaze
Your admiring entourage

Could you but know
Who formed your gleaming gown
And bequeathed to you
Your glorious distinctive robe
That you now allow to
Trail behind you
On the ground

Yet you appear
Oblivious
As to how or when
Or who
And are quite content to be
Simply and most gloriously
A peacock

ON MY BIRTHDAY

My My My!
The years do fly
The pace once thought benign
But that was long before
There were
Quite so many more

I must confess
All the same
A certain gain
In making it thus far
Arriving at four score
And five
Still alive
With faculties and hair
Most still there
Intact

So on this my
Natal celebration
(which will scarcely stir
The Nation)
I am grateful once again
To arrive
With so much more
Than my scant virtue
Could attain

But then
I know

By grace we live
By grace we go
I am aware
I shall not linger here forever
So

I bid you join
As good friends do
To raise a cup and tarry
To sing a song
Laugh awhile
And as good friends
Make merry

For on my birthday
I declare
We need not weep
Or ponder
But rejoice that I have
Seen this day
Before departing
Yonder

So thank you, friends
From near and far
For coming to my party
You are my treasure
And my joy
And I am at
Your pleasure

I OFFER YOU MY HAND

I offer you my hand
The adventure is for friends
Of more than ordinary daring
Unafraid to risk tomorrow
Or share their dreams
Or touch the warmth and splendor
That waits to blossom and unfold
Where they come together

I SOMETIMES WONDER

We met
Strangers
But bridging yet
A chasm with
A smile
And words
A few
And then
In some small flicker
Of the heart
I knew

A kindling within
A warm curiosity
Touching old
Almost forgotten memories
Of other times and
Other faces
Precious too
Though swallowed by
Passing years

And so I wonder
Now and then
In this world that
Properly allows
But "one true love"
If perhaps
We are not blinded
By such stern propriety
And cannot see
A world that is
Indeed well supplied

With those who
Like the stranger with
The smile
If chance and fate
Were kind
Might reach across
The chasm that divides
And kindle
Yet again
The lovely flame
That makes of
Passing strangers
Beloved friends

OUR STREET

Turn in where you see
The gate
Where one large tree
With leafy arms spread wide
Stands guard

You will find us
Not far down this
Ordinary lane
Bordered by small dwellings
Much like ours
Though perhaps
Not quite the same

For there are differences
Here and there
"Distinctions" some might say
Visible to a careful eye
That notes such things
As they gaze about
While passing this way

All these echo I suppose
The different folks who
Dwell within
So alike in many ways
Yet different too
Each within their own
Distinctive skin

While all drive down this
One familiar lane
And smile and greet each other
In our passing by
At times a memory occurs
And with it comes a sigh

For other faces we once knew
Who lived just down the way
Once smiled and said their
Bright hello
In what is now
A quickly fading
Yesterday

So we drift down this
Well traveled lane
Conscious that our time to greet
Will someday pass to others
Who will dwell
On this
Our old
Familiar street

REDEMPTION

I was wounded
Where I could not bleed
In the blood of
More usual wounds
Though heart wounds are
More lasting
And sometimes leave
Indelible scars

But then
The hand of love
Lay gently on the place
And soothed the
Fever of my pain
Until
At last
I was whole again

LET THE SILVER YEAR SHINE

So it's twenty five for us
Who could have planned!
And to be alive and
Celebrate with you
Is a blessing most amazing
I'm sure you understand

For you, my dear,
Like years gone on before
A cause for real thanksgiving
And each year that we share
Better than the last
And with more reason
To love you that much more

Your love spelled out
In all the common tasks you do
You cook and wash and clean and plan
And cap the finished ironing with
A smile and lovely hug for me
How grand!

So this brief word
Is penned to let you know
This quarter century of life we share
Finds me still much in love with you
For all the many ways you've shown your love
Throughout our really
Quite amazing years

THANKFUL

There is no better word to sum up
All you mean to me
And to so many others
Truth be told
Yet none can mean it more than I
For the countless ways you are
And have been a blessing
Since you became
My remarkable wife!

On this, your birthday,
Your special celebration
(They should have saved the
Fireworks for now)
I humbly pause to pen
These words of gratitude
Beyond what words can say
Yet in profound thankfulness
To you, dear Bev,
And to Gracious Providence
For the daily blessing
Your presence in my life provides

There are so many ways
Beyond all measure
Your steady
Steadfast love
Displayed in ways
Both large and small
Undergirds our life together
And most surely brightens
This world we share

THOUGHTS AT ALMOST EIGHT
(KNIGHTWATCH)

The ceiling fan
Whirrs and breathes
Soft upon my head
As slowly ticks
The office clock
Measuring
The moments remaining
Until
I head for home

And thus
Awaiting
I will perchance find
A cup of tea
A cookie or two
Before
I go
To bed

THE HALLOWED PLACE

There is a place
A hallowed place
I keep within
Quiet
With an air
Almost Holy

On its walls
If walls they be
Are pictures
Countless
Treasured
Of those I loved
And love
Scenes
Of ordinary days
Yet magical
For all they were
To me

To that place
That hallowed place
I retire
When dark days descend
Or life becomes
Too bleak

Until
In heaven's time
Soul refreshed
Washed clean
I emerge to find
A brighter sun
Fresh dawning
And all life
Holy

THE COMING OF PEACE

The rumble in the west subsides
The chaos rolls away
The battle's won, the foe undone
And someone shouts "hurray!"

Hurray indeed, oh simple child
Upon our knees we go
In thankfulness that God
So blessed
His people here below

But oh remember eager one
At what great price this day
Was bought from out the
Hands of death
Too great, too dear to pay

The sea now rolls by island shoals
As blue as e'er before
Though in her breast
Our dear ones rest
Beyond the last great door

There's land across the sea
Behold
Less favored than our own
Where furrowed by
The wheels of war
A million dreams are sown

Grain shall grow and ripen there
And children laugh and play
While cannon rust to harmless dust
Which spoke death yesterday
But may the farmer ponder long
When plowing in the land
His peaceful blade unearths again
A work of war's grim hand

Nor e'er forget
Though time erase
The broken walls of war
A million dreams that yesterday
The future held in store
Are sown within his native land
Nor rise to greet the spring
But wait the coming of the
Prince of Peace
The Savior and the King

And these shall trust that
In our hearts
Their passing will yet cry
Remember us! Remember us!
And for the future try

To love ye one another so
That men may dwell with men
In peace with charity for all
You may forget us then

WARREN

It all began
Many years ago
When he and I were young
In college days at U.S.C.
Our lives had just begun

He shared his fervent faith with me
And I shared mine with him
Bonding over many things
Cars, football games and girls
And prospects great
Or slim

But my dear friend was more
Than just the sum
Of college joy and youthful fun
For God had called
"Warren, I need you"
When he answered, "Here am I"
New life had begun

Seminary and to life beyond
Into the thick of things he went
Giving every call his best
From Pittsburg to Westminster
Wherever he was sent

With dear Jane by his side
The years wore on
They lived and loved
And shared the path
'Til at last
Time slowed Warren's rapid stride

He was a solid sort of friend
Who planned things in advance
More than once we traveled
Visiting Chateaux and wineries
Tasting the best of France

But it was Warren's observation
That life had a funny side
And he kept a catalogue of fun
To share with those who
Need a smile
To breast life's awesome tide

We often remembered days
Long gone
Warren did and I
The songs we sang
The friends we loved
And even what it might mean
To die

But this he knew, my old friend did,
The future holds a shining
Guarantee
The Savior has a promise given
There will be a place for us
A blessed place
Beyond a shining sea

So when at last, his battle won,
Warren simply slept away
His "bucket list" full to the brim
Heaven
Had begun

WHEN A FRIEND IS VERY ILL

Help!
We cry
And when it comes
Hurrying down the hall
White robed
Stethoscope and all
What then?
When life runs so very low
Help seems
Helpless
And even as we pray
We wonder
Is it later than we know?

Not that we really believe
There is some divine clock
In a far off sky
Such thoughts long since
Ceased to comfort
But as we stand beside the bed
Of one so gravely ill
Our thoughts must probe the
Deeper questions
We are so often ill disposed
To ponder

Yet a simple truth
Hangs clearly
In the room's quiet air:
Life is a gift
Filled with beauty, wonder,
Possibility and
Limitations
And somewhere
Somehow
Someday
An ending
And we do not know
Here at bedside
What time it is

Yet
Somehow we dare believe
Our mortality
Is but prelude
To an infinite "More"
And our beloved friend
Lies somewhere nearer
The answer to
Our questions
Than we who stand in
Silent awe and sorrow
By the quiet bed

The only help we can give
Just now
Lies in
Loving
Caring
And perhaps a silent touch
That says:
You do not face this hour alone
The journey
Should you face it now
Is yours to take
As someday ours will be
But our spirits
Buoyed by love
Will go with you
While in our hearts you
Will live on
And someday, somewhere
We do believe
We shall meet again

Section 5

Senior Years

A GENTLE MIND

O for a gentle mind
That lets the rasp of
Time and circumstance
Hone away
Rough edges of
Harsh judgments
That too often
Have led my thoughts astray

Some I love and treasure
And hold dear
Whose hopes and dreams
My credulity finds fanciful
Or strange
Noble souls
Whose passions rise and
Hearts embrace
Causes for which I find
No inner voice commanding

Yet for us all this
Mortal limitation
Life's incessant
Every day reminds
That what appears so
Right and true today
May
Beneath time's unsparing hand
Find unexpected alteration
And in some unseen tomorrow Appear in an
Unexpected light

So let my mind
As time slips by
Grow gentle with the passing years
Rejoice in beauty everywhere
Sink deep roots deeply
In the ground
Of love and kindness
Everywhere
Nor fail the light that
Mercy sheds
In every land and clime

So may I may find
At last
A more wise and kind
A more
Gentle mind

A RELAXING DAY

Now and then there
Comes a day
With nothing much to do
That is really pressing
That allows me sit
Coffee cup in hand and
Read the morning paper
I think you understand

With no visitor in sight just now
Attire remains an option
And my pajamas somehow seem
All right today
After all
I'm not a main attraction

Slippers in the closet rest
And my comfy socks
Will fill the bill just right
Until I stretch and yawn
And bid you all
Goodnight

So I recline in this chair old
Like me with groans and squeaks
And sip my coffee
While I read the news
But
O my gosh
This is last week's!

Oh well
My relaxing day
Is not a calendar affair
And news that's old
Like news that's new
Has always much to say

But when my coffee's done
And I have drained my cup
I'll settle back and take a nap
Until someone comes along
And says
"Wake up!"

AT EVENTIDE

As slows the day
And twilight softens
And restfulness comes on
Dear God of each day's length
Who sees the end
From the beginning
I turn again to thy dear arms
While my ever trusting soul
Awaits thy bidding

For the swiftly passing years
Have been rich with blessing
And my heart
Is full and overflowing
With the goodness of my God!

And so
Dear Father
At life's eventide
I lay me down to rest
Perhaps to wake
Beyond the silver morning
Home at last
In that long awaited place
Where all is loveliness
And peace
And earth's eventide gives way
To Heaven's greater dawn

CHECK LIST

Numbers one and two
Check
But three and four
One must admit
Do leave
A bit
To be
Desired

So it's best
To put the pencil down
Avoiding the temptation
To pretend an efficiency or zeal
Not yet attained

So it is with years
The bucket list of dreams
Still unfulfilled
Plans made
With magnificent intention and
Noble purpose surely
Only to evaporate with a sigh
"If only...."

The days slip by
The weeks, the months, the years
While calendar and clock record
Their silent judgement
So many opportunities slipped by
While procrastination ruled
And I
Took a brief
Nap

Yet
Even now I hear
One more call
One last glimmer of
Whatever yet might be

So listen carefully my heart
Lest circumstance or
Old habit
Deafen yet again
Divine communication

Let the aging bucket fill
Once more with dreams
Both splendid
And mature
So with what remains
Of time
Energy and vision
Grasp the fleeting hour
The day
The deed
And let life
Tho' even now at
Eventide
Begin

CONTENTMENT

Long lie the ancient hills
Low against the western sky
As wisps of cloud
Gentle as a fairy dream
Drift
Slowly
By

Long thoughts come easy
As I settle back
And rest
Letting all troubles of
This raucous world
Slide quietly off
My chest

A deep breath and then
A long, long sigh
Smiling in
Profound contentment
I let
The world
Go
By

Although my input is
Really not required
To make this earth rotate
I do confess that I
Once thought
I might enter
The debate

So grand the plans and
Deep the thoughts
Of those gone before
Who left their mark on
Great monuments
And certainly
Much more

But though without such summary
A humble soul
As evening closes down
Might still assess the losses
And the gains
This simple life
Has known

So now content with
No regrets
All sins forgiven
Great gratitude for all
I sit and watch
The setting sun
And hear the night bird call

So I shall hum a long-loved tune
And then
With deep, deep sigh
Welcome velvet night
And its promise
Of the
Coming dawn

THE CONTROVERSY

"I believe"
He said
With flaming eye
And voice that boomed
Like thunder
And not a soul on hearing
Could doubt
His stern intent

But then
Another rose
Quiet
And with
Unassuming air
Laid bare in
Measured tones
A truth
un-contradictable
Yet at odds
With what had
Gone before

So it went
And still it goes
With fervor fierce
Or perhaps
A quiet observation
The controversy
Continues
Until at last
All tongues silent
Our conversation
And our history
End

DAY'S JOURNEY

Step by step
Hour by fleeting hour
Moments mount
Like fast-flowing sand
Through the hourglass

Now
I ponder
Conscious of the heartbeat
Coursing blood through
Aging veins

So comes a
Quiet contemplation
Reminding me that
After all
I shall not live forever
Nor would I wish it
When flesh grows frail
And beauty fades
So even these eyes
Cannot behold
What yet remains

So let the hourglass run
'Til all its sands are sifted down
And it is time
To bid goodnight
Until timeless Heaven breaks
And the journey of forever
Has begun

GLORY SOMEDAY

Dear Father of my spirit
And the wind's wide arch
Should I fall before
This day is done
Let none of those I love
Mourn sorely or too much
Since I go to sky and wind
And your high heaven
Sunlit brimmed and singing!

Then I'll be glad, my Father
Glad, glad, glory-dazzled
Unbound and free!
To know at last the fountainhead
From which such visions, longings
Issued
To clasp again at last
Lost loves
To bosom and to heart

So it shall surely be
As my faith has believed
Unproved
Not really needing it
For those roses by the tilted step
Assure me quite enough
And your sky and wind-arch over
Are a mystic music
Singing in the smiling face of day
These enough
To let me rest

In peace
For should it be today
Or in some other
That great matriculation
Shall come
That glad, glad, glory-dazzled day!
Raptured to life's own
Warm, eternal heart
And your own
Someday

HOPE STILL SHINES

My mind still runs
Tho' steps are slower now
And the thought occurs that
I am mortal
Destined for dust

Ah but still
A deathless hope
Burns brightly just the same
That the grand adventure of
These fleeting years
Shall not end when
Breath is gone
And heart is still

The promise has been made
By one brief career
Like a streaking star
Left a path of light
Across the shadowed pages
Humanity has penned
And it is He indeed
Who had said
Life lived in God
Shall never end

So run my thoughts
Considering the passing hours
Wondering
If
The earthly story has
Not long
Before it finds its end
Yet the promise shines
And faith its trust declares
The adventure shall go on
The adventure shall go on

I AIN'T DONE YET

Don't write me off just yet
My friend
Though I got a pain or two
But that's what comes
Of livin' long
As a body oughta do

There's daybreak comes
With mornin' grub
An' coffee black as sin
They's chores awaitin'
At the barn
Them cows need
Bringin' in

Milikin' time an' hay to cut
Fence needs mendin' too
Combine needs
Some fixin' done
Which a feller
Oughta do

So whatever years
A feller's got
Don't matter much it seems
Ya just keep chorin'
To the end
An' be buried in your jeans

But I'm still lively, don't cha know
Full o' sap an' perkin'
Ain't done yet
An' you can bet
You'll find me out there
Workin'

I HURT

I hurt
No grievous wound
Most surely
Though stranger to
My carefree life
Save perchance
The usual ills of childhood
A dentist's drill or two
Or prick from a
Needful needle
Now and then

Perhaps
It is my time
To learn the lessons taught
By pain
Knowing that the Teacher
Planned it well
No day wasted
No hour gone by
Without some use
Though often
Belatedly perceived

Still
I hurt
And looking up
(Though doubtless down
Would do)
I ask the touch
That long ago
Healed the suppliant
By Galilee
And still today
Can erase away
My hurt
Minor though it be

I WONDER

I do wonder
Now and then
About the claims I hear
For this or that
Or might be
"You need to know, my dear"

Oh but then
The facts are trotted out
To make the case air-tight
The matter settled
Don't you see
For the fellow seated
Over there and
Smugly smiling
His delight

Still
I do wonder when
Another
With a dissenting view
May rise to offer facts ignored
Or perhaps unknown
To that fellow who
It must be said
Quite clearly had
No clue

So it does appear
Most wise to weigh
Each matter
In the light
That may be found on
Any given day
Or even late at night

Thus shall I leave
To unfolding hours their
Confirmation
Or negation
To put the stamp of truth
On all our conflict
And our learned
Disputation

So may I walk
In humility and hope
Through my remaining days
To gain what wisdom
May yet be found
From this life's complex
And beautiful
Though often
Quite confusing
Ways

IF ONLY WE COULD KNOW

Ah yes
If only
We could know
That this
Is so
Though not perhaps with
Certainty
Although something close
Might do

However
Appearances
At times deceive
Giving things a
Certain shape or size
And we arise
To fight or flee
Give thanks
Or weep
Though bitter tears
Won't often change
Reality

So
It seems
To be humble
Is really the best
Admitting that
Lacking crystal ball

Or prophet's divine vision
We must simply trust
Chancing
And in faith believing that
We will find
A path
Leading
Although by ways unsought
To an unexpected grace
Tomorrow

NIGHT SONG

Fleeting
The hours, the days
The years
Gone like a breath, a dream
Gone are the laughter
And the tears
That flow
In the firelight gleam

For dreams remain
Soul deep inside
Outshining the starlight bright
Recollections still throng
Like a well loved song
Once sung
On a starry night

Soul songs are sung
As the years fly by
Though most may never know
But the angels care
And their blessing share
With the silent bard
Below

So sing your song
To the night wind now
And know that the listening stars
Will hold it dear
In heaven's ear
Forever and ever
I know

WHAT WOULD IT BE

If only one last song
Were left to me
One final word to speak
Or pen
What would it be?

If but one more canvas
Left to fill
One poem to rhyme
One story to tell
Before there is
No more
What then?

Is what's been already spoken
Writ daily in life's everyday affairs
To be the sum and total
Recorded, tallied and combined
To tell emerging generations
This brief life had
Just this to say and
Nothing more?

Still
There is always
More!
More to perceive
Discover and proclaim
Taste
Taste and explore
More unraveling of the
Tight-wound ball

The mystery of life and love
Each finds
And struggles to embrace
Before
On an ordinary day
The final page is turned
Is writ upon
And the book
At last
Is closed

NOT FAR

I once seemed so
Very far
To journey's end
So many beckoning years
Left to travel
Before the sunset
And whatever then
Might be

Now
With so many years
And memories
Adventures of a lifetime
Logged in passing
Long thoughts do come
And leave me
Wondering

How many sunsets
There may be
Before the final night shall fall
And then?

Sunrise!
One may yet believe
Shining through whatever
Doubts may be
A new dawn awaits
And a wondrous
Beginning again

OLD MAN IN A CHAIR

He sits
Quietly staring
At the floor
Hands clasped
Wrinkled fingers that
Bear the signs of
A hard life's labor
In those yesterdays
That he yet remembers
Though he may not
Know your name today
Though you call him Dad

His eyes
Quiet now beneath
A shaggy brow
Once flashed with
Youthful fervor
For the things he believed
Were clearly right

But the years have seen the
Issues pass
As life moves on
And the world he knew
Has somehow vanished
Like smoke from a
Long extinguished fire
Leaving him sitting in
His old familiar
Chair

SOLITUDE

Alone
At this tiny table
Surrounded by couples
And whole families
Chattering and happy
Reminded once again
Of what it means to be
Alone

Across the room
An old man sits
Very much alive
(You can see it in his eyes)
In touch with all around
Though wrapped in quiet dignity
And the comfort of
His solitude

So I am reminded
That to be alone
Need not be a
Melancholy thing
But may instead allow
The lesson to unfold
Of what it means
To be
A solitary self
Wrapped in all the Many things
That belong to just
Being alive

Grant

THE BUTTON

She wears it 'round her neck
You see
So she'll be safe in case
She falls
Or other things
Of catastrophic vein occur
As well they might
When you are eighty four
Or more

But then
It dims her spirit not a whit
For with a twinkle in her eye
She celebrates
The treasurers that remain
The gifts of life
And love
That still she holds
The lilt
Of a long loved song
The dance of sunlight
On the water
A poem's gentle lift
And the ringing laughter
Of a child
These things she holds
And smiles
As memories throng

There is a message
In that grand old lady's face
Telling us
As life hastens on
To celebrate what remains to us
Until
At last
The book is closed

THE ENDING AND BEGINNING

On some ordinary day
If such there truly be
The unbidden word may come
And suddenly
Nothing is the same

Some switch in life's unseen heart
Is thrown
And what seemed a
Stationary world is different
In a fundamental way
A long accustomed dimension
A vital and important part
Of life is gone
The last page reached
The last line ended
A familiar and beloved book
Has closed
Forever

Yet
The question does arise
For which faith alone
The answer may provide
Is this journey truly done
Or is the ended story
Only just begun?

Are there horizons of the soul
Invisible in mortal years
Awaiting when the curtain falls
And earthly visions end in tears?

Is there a grand reunion
Waiting on another shore
When earthly life has ended
And a journey of
A different kind
Begun?

So may faith provide a
Shining vision
And a joyful hope inspire
That our ending may become
A birthing in Forever
And the beginning of a journey
On another, fairer shore

THE LONG VIEW

Today I paused to ponder
About tomorrow and the
Time beyond
If such there be for me
And if not
If my accumulated years should
Somehow sooner end
What then?

"It's been a good run"
A good friend said not long ago
Whose sum of years is
Close to mine
And I would echo that refrain
And add more
Wrapped in gratitude for all

But an old man's exercise in
Looking back along the path his
Life has taken
Brings many scenes to mind
Where not every choice was wise
And some were clearly
Quite mistaken

Still, when life's last trump
Shall sound
What truly matters more
Is to find the arms of God
Wide open
And sweet reunion waiting on
That farther shore

There I shall bow in
Most profound thanksgiving
That so very much was
Good indeed
Though not all of it was gain
And I must surely wiser be
From lessons learned
Through pain

Growing old is not a choice
Though what it means may be
Fading memory and hearing too
Are not without a modest remedy

As for me, I've found
Friendships grow more treasured
Through the years
Even as some regrettably must end
And I take consolation in the faith
That we shall somehow,
Somewhere meet again

Yes, some of us may wobble as
We go, perhaps assisted by
Walker or cane
While those younger or more agile
Still play golf or swim a mile
Yet it really doesn't matter
For all of it is gain

For what is treasured in the heart
Most surely matters most
To be shared along life's busy way
With the generation waiting
For which we older folks
Are host

THE NEXT STEP

I was walking
As brisk as aging muscles
Would allow
Watching where I placed my feet
On the aging asphalt street

For a crack I've spotted
Here and there
In this familiar lane
And codgers like the one
I have become
Could take a tumble
And quickly end
In the nearby
Urgent Care

So the thought somehow
Crossed my mind
That I'm not unlike
The street I view
Since my life has
Developed here and there
A crack or two!

At any one
A stumble might occur
And as someone counseled
I had best take care
And watch my step
Until my journey's done

So I'll keep plodding
Until all my plodding ends
Then sit back to savor
A glass of wine or two
With old and
Sedentary friends

THE TIDE

Slowly
As awakening from
A pleasant dream
I have become aware of
The moment
Of a tide
Though when I saw it
Did not see
It had much to do
With me

But now
A gentle but persistent wind
Begins to blow
Turning the pages of
The calendar
Much more quickly
Than they once did before

It is though
An unseen angel with
Outstretched wings
With piercing
Yet gentle eye
Breathed a holy breath
Upon the world
That moves
Both time and tide

So all things are carried
On its crest
To become or disappear
While days slip by
And time grows old
Making all we love
More dear

So it shall be
Someday
We shall reach
Our journey's end
Stepping through
A shining door
To find that God
Is as God has always been
Our Friend

WHEN IS BECOMES WAS

It seems to me
Upon reflection
As times moves on
Without what ought to be
Required reflection
Quite oft'n is lost
To our attention
The many things that came about
Some time ago
Through accident
Or may be
Through clever tinkering
And invention

The world moves on
In its many sided evolution
From fire and stone
To heaving seas in constant motion
And we evolved
Somewhere along the way
To alter much of that which is
So that we might have a say
As to
What our today might be
Which after all
Soon will be our
Yesterday

So do we dare to hope
Our children's children
Might declare
That we who once resided in
Their fast receding "was"
Didn't really do too badly
In those days before
And perhaps
Even
Assured a happier and
More livable "is"
Than ever had been before

WHERE OLD DREAMS GO

We have them
Stored Away
Securely locked in
Memory's old closet
Most gathering the
Gentle dust of
Forgetfulness
Though of course
Not all

Like a song once dear
Unsung for many years
That some chance note or
Passing tune may
Resurrect
While we
With a smile or
Even an errant tear
May break forth
In glad, nostalgic singing

Many a dream remains
Unshared
In memory's old closet
Too tender for now
And today's hard exposure

Yet remains
A memento of where
Our heart once dared to dream
A beauty that could
Never be
Yet treasured still
In precious memory

Section 6

Sketches

These sketches could not find a home in a poem. However, one may inspire you to write one of your own.

Grant

Granit

Grant

Grant

Grant

Printed in the United States
By Bookmasters